FORCE AND STRENGTH

Neil Ardley

Series consultant: Professor Eric Laithwaite

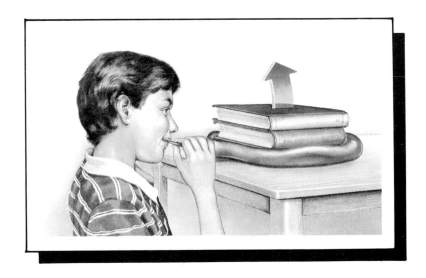

Franklin Watts

London   New York   Toronto   Sydney

The author
Neil Ardley gained a degree in science and worked as
a research chemist and patent agent before entering
publishing. He is now a full-time writer and is the
author of more than fifty information books on
science, natural history and music.

The consultant
Eric Laithwaite is Professor of Heavy Electrical
Engineering at Imperial College, London. A well-
known television personality and broadcaster, he is
best known for his inventions on linear motors.

© 1984 Franklin Watts Ltd

First published in Great
Britain in 1984 by
Franklin Watts Ltd
12a Golden Square
London W1

First published in the United
States of America by
Franklin Watts Inc.
387 Park Avenue South
New York
N.Y. 10016

Printed in Belgium

UK edition:
ISBN 0 86313 178 6
US edition:
ISBN 0-531-03777-0
Library of Congress
Catalog Card Number:
83-51443

Designed by
David Jefferis

Illustrated by Janos Marffy,
Hayward Art Group and
Arthur Tims

SILLY PUTTY® is a registered
trademark of Binney and
Smith Inc., used with
permission.

FORCE AND STRENGTH

Contents

Equipment

In addition to a few everyday items, you will need the following equipment to carry out the activities in this book.

Balloon or plastic bag
Books
Carton
Eggs (2)
Forks (2)
Knife
Matchbox and matches
Pencil
Plasticine

Poles or brooms (2)
Potato
Rice
Rope
Ruler
Silicone rubber
String
Tube (plastic or rubber)
Wire coat hanger

Introduction

Force and strength are an important part of
your life. Every time you move something,
you produce a force. Inside your body,
your heart never stops forcing blood around
to keep you alive. Your muscles and bones
are strong so that you can run and work
hard and also survive knocks and accidents.

However, it is not only movement that
makes use of force and strength. Forces
press on all structures, from a simple chair
to a huge building. The structures must be
made of strong materials connected
together in such a way that they can
withstand these forces and remain standing.

By doing the activities in this book, you
will begin to gain an understanding of force
and strength. Several of the activities show
you ways of exerting powerful forces and of
appearing to be very strong. There are also
some tricks that use force in unusual ways.
Take care with experiments that involve
pulling or pushing people or things. Do not
hurt yourself or others.

✳ This symbol appears throughout the
book. It shows you where to find a
scientific explanation for each activity.

Strength and weakness

Some materials are stronger than they seem and others are weaker.

Paper or potato?

Take a piece of paper and a potato. Ask a friend which is stronger—the paper or the potato? To find out, fold the paper in two and wrap it around a knife as shown. Then push the wrapped knife firmly down into the potato. It slices through the potato without cutting the paper!

✳ The piece of paper is stronger than the potato because the tiny molecules inside the paper grip one another with more force than the molecules in the potato. It is harder to separate the paper molecules than the potato molecules, so the knife slices the potato instead of the paper.

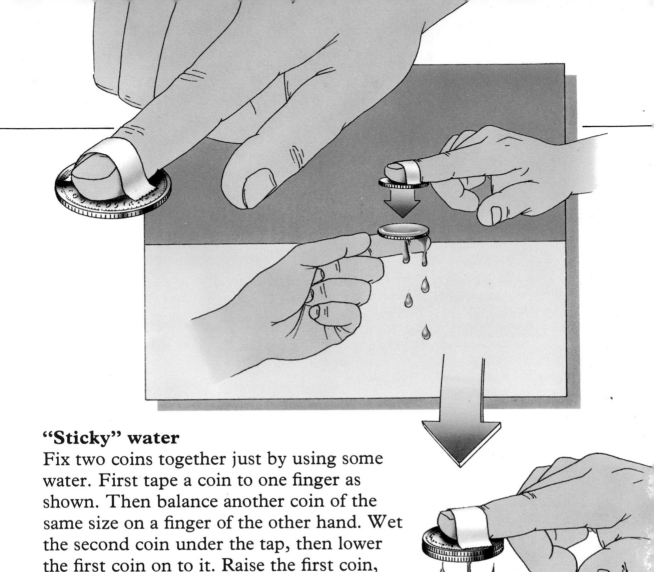

"Sticky" water

Fix two coins together just by using some water. First tape a coin to one finger as shown. Then balance another coin of the same size on a finger of the other hand. Wet the second coin under the tap, then lower the first coin on to it. Raise the first coin, and the second coin will stick to it.

✳ Water molecules grip each other loosely, so water is not strong. The molecules easily attach themselves to other kinds of molecules, which is why things get wet. The water molecules grip the metal molecules on the surfaces of the coins. This makes the water fill the space between the coins so that air cannot get in. The pressure of the air then holds the coins together.

△ Make sure that the coins get really wet, and put them together carefully. Try again if you do not succeed in sticking the coins together first time.

Continued overleaf

Silly putty

Take a piece of silicone rubber, which you can mold into shape like plasticine. Pull it apart slowly and it stretches out like chewing gum. But pull it hard and it snaps. Then roll the piece into a ball and drop it. The silicone is now resilient and bounces. But hit it with a hammer and it shatters!

✳ Silicone rubber is a very unusual material. It can be weak, strong, soft or hard, depending on how much force you apply to it. If you use a lot of force, silicone rubber becomes brittle like glass and snaps and shatters. With less force, it becomes flexible like true rubber and will bend or bounce.

▽ You may be able to buy silicone rubber under the name of silly putty. If you cannot find any, try plasticine instead. It will not shatter under a hammer, but otherwise it behaves in a similar way.

Materials are strong when compressed because their molecules are forced closer together and grip each other more firmly. When a material is pulled or stretched, the molecules grip less firmly and it becomes weaker.

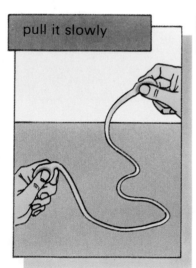

pull it slowly

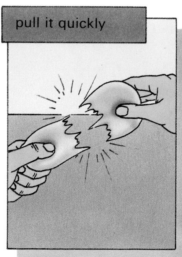

pull it quickly

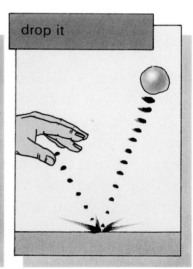

drop it

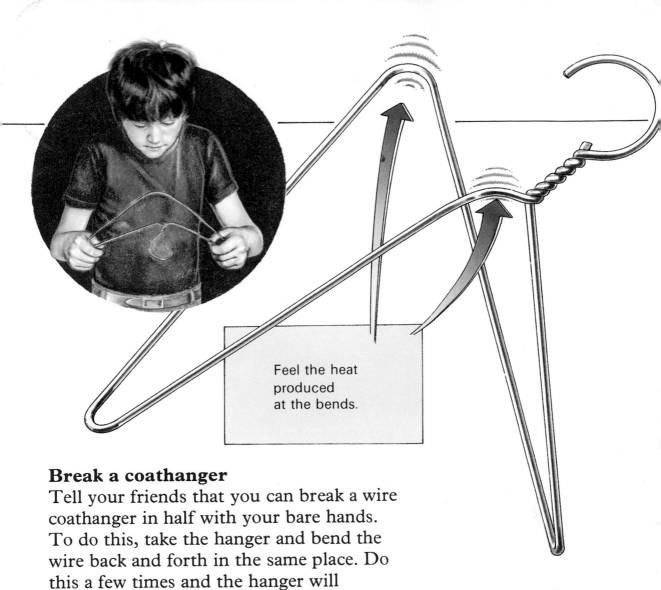

Feel the heat
produced
at the bends.

Break a coathanger

Tell your friends that you can break a wire
coathanger in half with your bare hands.
To do this, take the hanger and bend the
wire back and forth in the same place. Do
this a few times and the hanger will
suddenly snap. Touch the place where it
has broken. It is very hot.

△ Keep the pieces as
they can be used in the
experiment on page 26.

The particles of steel inside the wire
are gradually pulled apart as you bend the
wire. This causes the steel to change. It
begins to get brittle, like glass, and
eventually the wire snaps. The wire gets
hot because the particles rub against each
other as the wire is bent.

Strong structures

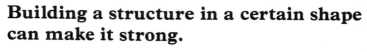

Building a structure in a certain shape can make it strong.

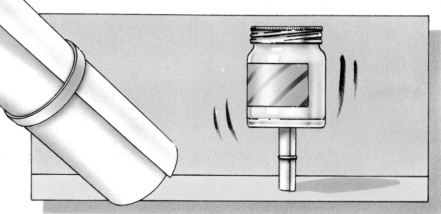

Tough tube

Make a piece of paper strong enough to support a heavy weight. Use a piece of writing paper that is new and fairly stiff. Roll the paper into a tube and secure it with a rubber band. Then place different objects on top. The paper tube will support a heavy weight before it buckles out of shape. Oil rigs have tubular legs for strength.

✺ A structure that is cylindrical in shape, like the paper tube, is strong. It cannot collapse easily because the sides of the tube cannot bend in two directions at the same time. This makes the structure rigid.

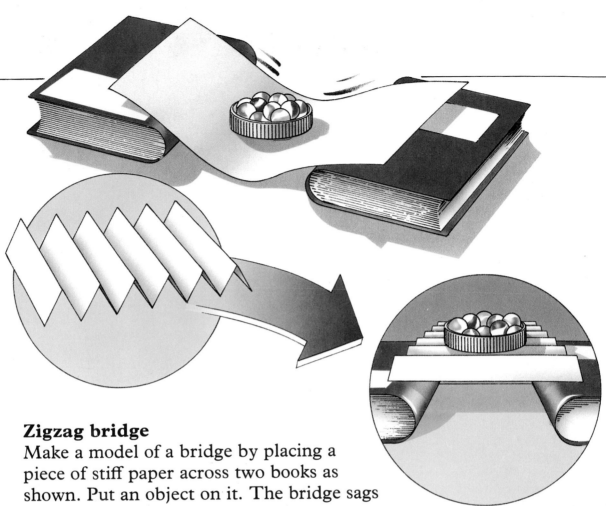

Zigzag bridge

Make a model of a bridge by placing a piece of stiff paper across two books as shown. Put an object on it. The bridge sags or even collapses under the weight. Now bend the paper into a zigzag shape and try again. This time the model bridge will support a much heavier object.

△ Use a lid and marbles to test the strength of the model bridges. See how many marbles each bridge will support.

✹ The first bridge collapses because the paper is flat. Under the weight, it bends easily in a downward direction. The zigzag bridge is much stronger because of its shape. Like the tube on the opposite page, the sides of each zigzag cannot bend in the same direction as the weight pushes down.

Continued *overleaf*

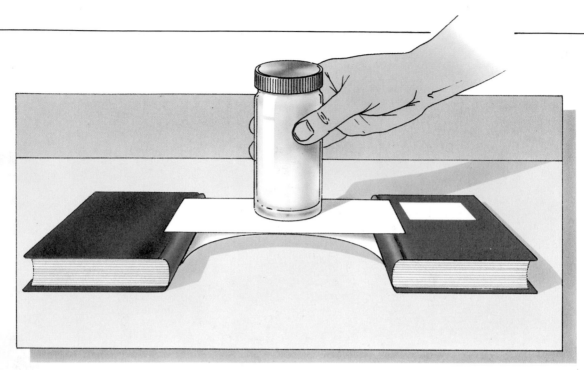

▽ Arch dams can be built with high and thin walls because the arch shape is so strong. The pressure of the water behind the dam compresses the arch and the concrete is very strong in compression.

Arches for strength

Make the first model bridge shown on page 11. See how it sags or collapses, even beneath a light object. Now take the piece of paper, bend it into an arch and place it between the books so that it supports a paper bridge as shown. This model arch bridge will now support a heavy object.

✳ The weight of the object on the arch pushes the arch in on itself. This compresses the paper, and paper is strong in compression. An arch is a very strong structure when used in this way. This is why many bridges are built in an arch shape.

As strong as eggs

Hard boil two eggs by boiling them for at least five minutes. Then cool the eggs and carefully cut them both in half. Remove the insides and place the four half shells upsidedown on a table. Now pile up books on top of the shells. Even though the eggs are so fragile, they will support several books.

✺ Like an arch, a shell is strong from outside because a force pushing on the shell compresses it. This is why the half shells support the books. But when pushed from inside, a shell is weak because it is not compressed. A bird is therefore protected from outside forces inside the shell, but can break the shell when it hatches.

△ Using a knife with a serrated (saw-tooth) edge, cut each hard-boiled egg slowly and carefully in half.

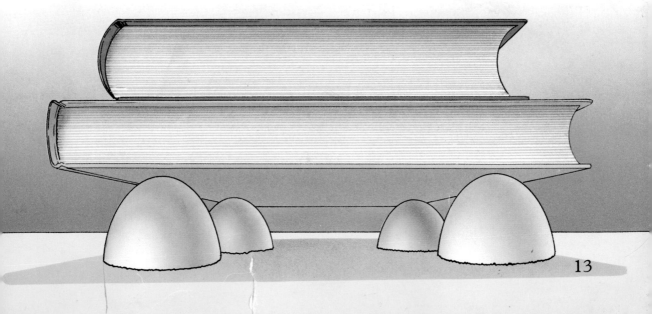

Forces in balance

All the forces in a standing structure always balance one another.

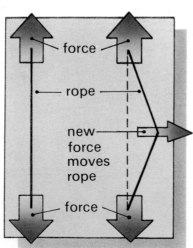

▽ The new force makes the rope move until the forces balance again.

force

rope

new force moves rope

force

Strong-arm tactics

Three people are needed for this experiment. Two of them hold a rope and pull on it. They should pull hard but equally so that they do not move. The third person now stands in the middle and pulls on the rope. Even a light pull in the middle will make the rope move to one side.

✸ The first two people pull in opposite directions with equal strength, so their forces balance and they do not move. When the third person exerts a new force on the rope by pulling it, the rope moves until all three forces balance each other.

Super strength?

Several people can do this experiment. One person leans against a wall with arms out straight. The others stand behind in a line and push against the person in front. Even though they all push hard, they are unlikely to overcome the first person's strength and force him or her into the wall!

 As the first person pushes against the wall, the wall exerts a balancing force back. Each person pushes on the person in front. But the person in front also exerts a balancing force back on the person behind. All these forces balance each other, so no movement occurs.

Continued overleaf

Circular centipede

Get as many people together as you can find. Ask them all to stand in a circle. Then on your command, everyone should sit down at exactly the same time. If each person sits on the knees of the person behind, nobody will fall over. But everyone should then get up at the same time.

▽ If everyone in the circle shuffles their legs, the circle will rotate like a circular centipede. The world record for circular sitting like this is over 10,000 people.

✳ When each person sits, the legs of the person behind take their weight in the same way as a chair. The ground exerts a balancing force on their feet and the circle of people does not collapse.

Center of gravity

If your center of gravity is out of place you are helpless!

Chairbound

Sit in a chair with your back upright and your arms by your sides. Make sure that your feet are not under the chair. Now, keeping your back straight and *without* moving your arms, try to get up. You will not be able to do so, no matter how hard you try. Then stretch out your arms and try again. This time, you rise easily.

✳ When you are sitting with your arms down, you center of gravity is not above your feet. It pulls you back as you try to rise. When you stretch out your arms, you move your center of gravity above your feet. It no longer pulls you back, so you can rise.

△ Your center of gravity is a point at which all the weight of your body acts. Its position depends on the shape of your body. If it is not directly above your feet but outside them, you fall over. This is the case when you are sitting on a chair but the chair stops you falling. When you get out of a chair, you bring back your feet or bend your body forward so that your center of gravity is directly above your feet. You can then get up without falling over.

Continued overleaf

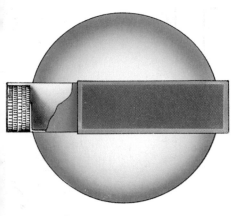

△ Use sticky tape to hold the coins in position inside the box. Place the coins as near to the end of the box as possible.

Magic matchbox

Take a matchbox and remove the matches. Then stick some coins to one end of the tray as shown. Tell a friend that you can make the matchbox balance right on the edge of a table. To do so, place the heavy end on the edge of the table. The matchbox will remain there without falling off.

✻ Without the coins, the center of gravity of the matchbox is in the middle of the box. The weight of the coins shifts the center of gravity toward the end of the box. The box will stay on the table if its center of gravity is above the table, otherwise it will fall off the edge.

Keeping upright

Place the matchbox with the coins on one end and tip it with a finger. Turn it upsidedown and try again. In one position, the box falls over easily but in the other, it often tips back and stays upright.

✳ If the box is placed on its heavy end, its center of gravity is near the base. Unless the box is tipped a lot, the center of gravity remains above the base and pulls the box back. When the box is turned upsidedown, the center of gravity is near the top end. Tipping it by only a small amount moves the center of gravity outside the base of the box and it falls over.

△ Any object with a center of gravity that is low down has to be tipped steeply before it falls over. Cars and other vehicles are built wide and low so that their center of gravity is always within the wheels. Then if they should tip for any reason, they will fall back on to their wheels.

Fun with forces

△ High-wire performers often carry a long pole. The pole lowers their center of gravity so that it is easier for them to stay on the wire. In addition, the pole helps to steady the performer because it takes a lot of force to move a heavy pole.

The action of forces can make things behave in unexpected ways.

Balancing act

Make a ball of plasticine about 1½ in (4 cm) across. Push a small nail or pin into it so that the point sticks out. Then insert two large forks into the plasticine as shown. Place the point on the top of a bottle and tip or push the forks. The construction will balance on the point, swinging back and forth or spinning around and around. It will not fall off the bottle top.

✸ The weight of the forks places the center of gravity of the whole construction under the point of the nail or pin. The point is pulled down on to the bottle top, so it cannot fall off.

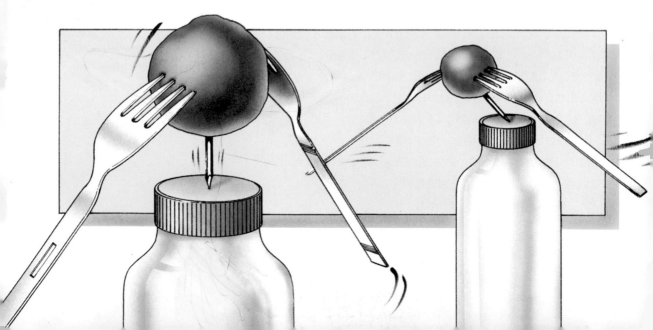

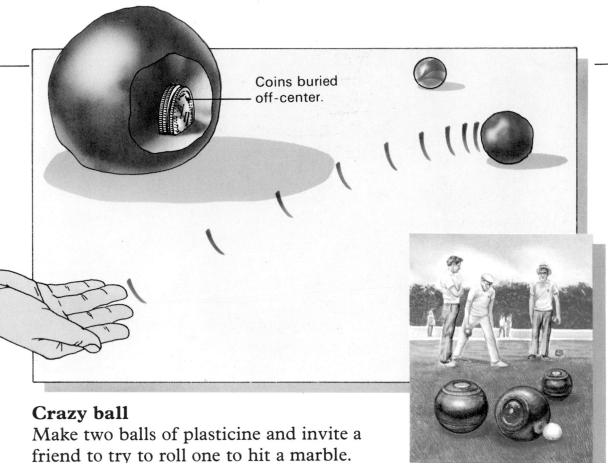

Coins buried off-center.

Crazy ball

Make two balls of plasticine and invite a friend to try to roll one to hit a marble. Without the other person seeing, push some coins into their ball. Place the coins off-center in the ball. Your ball will roll straight, but the other ball will usually swerve to one side!

✳ When the other person rolls their ball, it swerves if the buried coins are placed to one side of the ball. This happens because the weight of the coins produces a force that makes the ball swerve. When you roll your ball, the weight is even throughout so it rolls straight.

△ In the game of bowls, the balls are weighted unevenly so that they swerve as they roll. The players have to try and get them as near to the small white ball as they can.

21

Increasing forces

With simple devices like levers, use your strength to produce more force.

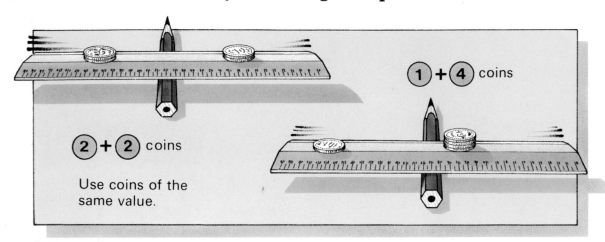

(1) + (4) coins

(2) + (2) coins

Use coins of the same value.

△ One coin placed at the end of the ruler produces the same amount of force as two coins halfway from the middle to the end, or four coins a quarter of the way from the pivot to the end. We use levers in devices like crowbars, wrenches or nutcrackers to increase our own strength. The amount of force we get is bigger if we pull or push on the lever at a greater distance from its pivot.

How a lever works

Tape a pencil to the middle of a ruler so that the ruler just balances when it rests on the pencil. Place piles of coins between the pencil and the ends of the ruler. Move them various distances from the pencil and change the number of coins in each pile. Find which combinations make the ruler balance.

✳ The ruler is a lever. The tilting force produced on each side depends on the weight of the coins multiplied by the distance of the coins from the pencil or pivot. If the tilting forces are the same, the ruler will balance.

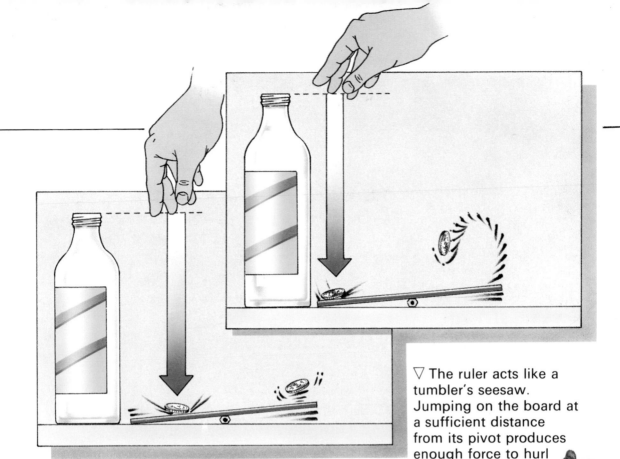

△ The ruler acts like a tumbler's seesaw. Jumping on the board at a sufficient distance from its pivot produces enough force to hurl people in the air.

Tumbler's seesaw

Take the ruler and pencil used in the last experiment and place a coin on one end. Now drop a coin on the other side of the ruler. The other coin will jump. Try again, dropping the coin from the same height, but making it strike the ruler at a greater distance from the pencil pivot. The first coin jumps higher.

✳ Because it falls from the same height each time, the coin strikes the ruler with the same force. But it produces more force at the other end if it hits the ruler at a greater distance from the pivot. This sends the first coin higher in the air.

Continued *overleaf*

▽ Arms, legs, hands, feet, fingers and toes all work as levers to increase the power of our muscles when we use them. If we can extend their length, we can apply more force with them. We do this with our arms when we use a hammer, for example, as well as when playing tennis or baseball.

Big hitter

Take a ball. Throw it into the air and hit it with your hand as if you were playing tennis. Note how far it goes. Try again but use a racket or bat. The ball should now travel a much greater distance.

✳ Your arm is a lever. The elbow is the pivot and the arm muscles provide the force. You cannot produce much force to drive the ball with your hand because it is near your elbow. The racket or bat is farther from your elbow so a greater amount of force is produced. It drives the ball a greater distance.

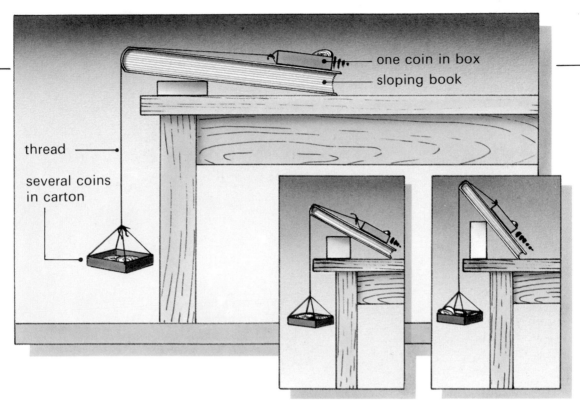

one coin in box
sloping book
thread
several coins in carton

Lifting power

Fasten a carton to a matchbox tray with some thread. Hang the thread over a sloping book as shown. Place a coin in the matchbox and add coins to the carton until it starts to pull the matchbox up the slope. Make the slope of the book steeper. More coins are now needed to move the box.

✳ If the slope is gradual, the box does not rise much in height as the carton descends. Little force is needed to raise the box, so fewer coins are required. Screws work in a similar way. You exert little force as you turn the screw, but the screw moves forward a short distance with a lot of force.

▽ As you turn the handle of a jack, your hand moves a long distance with little effort. A screw in the jack moves a short distance with great force, lifting the car.

25

Pulleys

pole

string

thread spool

bent wire

26

height raised

Pulleys enable you to lift heavy weights with little effort.

Measure the distance you pull the string.

Simple pulley

Fill a carton with marbles and feel how heavy it is. Attach the carton to a simple pulley as shown. Pull the string to lift the carton. The carton feels only half as heavy as before. Measure how much string you pull and how far the carton rises from the ground. The length of string pulled is twice the height that the carton rises.

✳ Because you pull the string through twice the distance that you raise the carton, you exert only half the force that you normally need to lift it. Real pulleys have wheels and ropes to reduce effort in this way.

Irresistible force

Loop a long rope several times around two poles or broom handles as shown. Two people then hold the poles apart with all their strength while a third person grips the rope and tries to pull them together. The two people holding the poles will not be able to resist the force pulling them together.

✳ The two poles and rope act like a pulley. The third person has to pull in a long length of rope to move the poles a little closer. The third person therefore does not have to exert much effort to overcome the strength of the first two people.

▽ Try to keep the two poles or handles parallel.

27

Pressure power

Applying pressure can provide enormous power with very little effort.

Blow up

Tell a friend you can lift a heavy object just by the power of your lungs. To do so, lay a large deflated balloon on a table and place the object on top. Then just blow into the balloon. The object will begin to rise, even without blowing very hard.

✳ As you blow up the balloon, every part of it beneath the object pushes upward. The amount of force that is produced depends on the pressure of the air. The air from your lungs has enough pressure so that over the whole object, enough force is produced to lift the object.

▽ Try lifting books in this way. You can add more books to find out how many you can raise. If you do not have a balloon or find a balloon too difficult to blow up, use a plastic bag instead.

Water lift

Fasten a tube to the balloon or bag used in the last experiment. Then pour water into it using a funnel. Keep the funnel above the object, and the water will enter the balloon and lift the object. Try pressing on the balloon to push the water back up the tube. Feel how much force you have to exert to make it rise at all.

✳ The pressure of the water in the balloon depends on the height of water in the tube. A low pressure is enough to lift the object. The water therefore continues to flow down the tube and into the balloon, raising the object more and more.

△ Use a rubber band to fix the tube into the neck of the balloon or plastic bag. Hydraulic machines such as braking systems contain a liquid under pressure like the water in the tube. The liquid pushes on a piston producing great power to operate the machine.

More force and strength

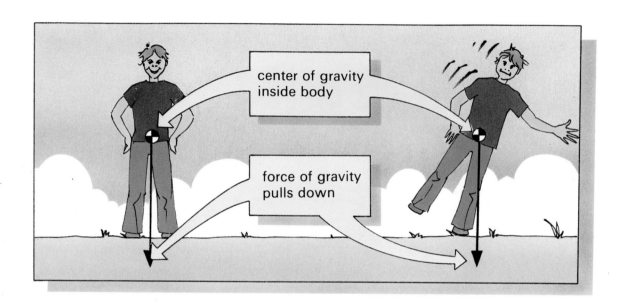

center of gravity
inside body

force of gravity
pulls down

△ Your center of gravity is somewhere inside the middle of your body. To stand up, your center of gravity must be directly above or within your feet (left). If you bend so that your center of gravity moves outside your feet (right), then you fall over. Wrestlers try to make their opponents fall by moving their center of gravity in this way.

Center of gravity
The center of gravity of an object is the point at which the force of gravity pulls on the whole object. If you can place a pivot beneath the center of gravity, then the object will balance on the pivot. In an object that is symmetrical, for example an object with a square or circular shape, then the center of gravity is at the center. But if the object is heavier or larger on one side, then its center of gravity is toward this side.

Force
When you push anything, you exert a force on it. Engines also produce a force to move something, and the force of gravity acts on all objects. If no other force resists these forces, then movement occurs. You pedal a bicycle, an engine powers a car or an object falls, for example. But if another force pushes against the first force, the two forces may cancel each other out so that no force operates. This happens with anything that is not

moving. A balancing force in the ground or the floor stops the force of gravity from moving it. However, the object must be strong enough to withstand the forces.

Levers

A lever increases the force you can produce on an object. The lever has a pivot about which it turns. You hold one end of the lever and apply a force called the effort, as in lifting a wheelbarrow or turning a wrench. At or near the pivot, a greater force, called the load, is produced. This is because the effort is farther away from the pivot than the load. However, the effort has to move a greater distance than the load. In levers of all kinds and devices like pulleys and jacks, a small force moving a big distance produces a large force moving a short distance.

Molecules

All things are made of tiny molecules. The molecules all pull on

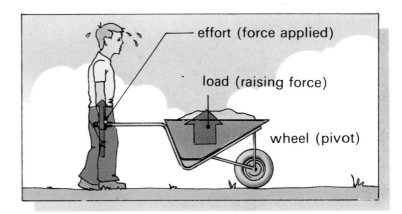

effort (force applied)

load (raising force)

wheel (pivot)

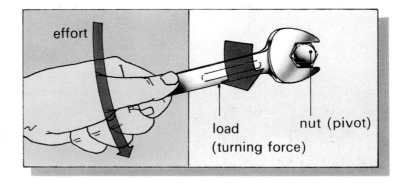

effort

load (turning force)

nut (pivot)

each other with a strong force. This force holds the molecules together, and gives a substance or material its strength.

Pressure

The pressure of a liquid or gas makes it exert a force on the walls of its container. If the pressure is greater, the liquid or gas pushes

△ A wrench and a wheelbarrow are kinds of levers. The force of your effort has to move a long distance in order to produce the stronger force or load that turns the nut or lifts the heavy weight of the wheel-barrow.

each part of its container with more force.

Index